STILL LIFE

STILL LIFE

poems

KATHERINE J. WILLIAMS

Cherry Grove Collections

Published by Cherry Grove Collections
P.O. Box 541106
Cincinnati, OH 45254-1106

ISBN: 9781625494177

Poetry Editor: Kevin Walzer
Business Editor: Lori Jareo

Visit us on the web at www.cherry-grove.com

For Sarah and Rachel

In memory of Shedd Williams
1935 – 1992

Acknowledgments

Christian Century: "Labyrinth" (as "Walking the Labyrinth") & "In Quarantine, Listening to the News"

Circle Yoga: "If Loneliness Were a Territory"

Delmarva Review: "Because of the Other" & "Old Woman Walking"

Entelechy International: "Letter to My Friend David Budbill" (as "Gloves")

Passager: "April 2020"

Poet Lore: "Before the First Knife"

Psaltery and Lyre: "Suppose There Were Light"

The Broadkill Review: "Assisted Living", "Evensong", "Ghost Pipes", "Late August, Lake Champlain"

The Northern Virginia Review: "Cicada" & "My Father's Hands"

Third Wednesday: "Blue Roan", "Savage Arms", "Rain"

Voices: "Blooms" (as "Bachelard Was Wrong"), "First Light and Lilies", & "Evening on Barr Hill"

"Miss Brown's Illustrative Materials" & "Slicing the Orange" appear in *Saying Goodbye To Our Mothers for the Last Time.*

"Still Life", "The Idea of Skin", & "Resurrection" appear in *The Widows' Handbook.*

"Conversation with Blake" & "Choices" appear in *The Poet's Cookbook.*

"The Dog Body of My Soul" appears in *How to Love the World: Poems of Gratitude and Hope.*

TABLE OF CONTENTS

III

IV

...it was like that, and after that, it was still like that, only all the time.

— Marie Howe

PROLOGUE

On Visiting My Husband
the Anthropologist in South Africa

In the middle of the night
on the other side of the world, flickering
light candles the hut, casting shadows
on the close sweet straw strewn
across dirt smoothed hard
by bare feet circling to call
the ancestors down. I lean against
the cool wall, melting into the warm
dark of arms beside me. He's here,
too, across the expanse of bodies, intent
on the ritual, not sensing the candles
dwindle. Alone in the swirling
eddy of the dance, I try not to think
of the incipient fire my mind
ignites, while the worshippers
weave into *kairos*, that moment out of time,
when something new flames into being.

THE LAST DAY

We walk, bundled, our breath
parting the sea of cold that closes in.
Free of the current of wills
that sometimes runs between us,
we lean into each other. We have time,
we say, so amble slowly block by block,
until he falls away from me.

The sudden intimacy of sidewalk, feet
of strangers. I think he's still holding
my hand until I sense I'm clutching his.
Busy people of all sorts slow down
and form a shield around us.

At Bellevue, the policeman dials
my daughter's number. A nurse appears,
hands me his wallet, tells me to wait.
She says they can't remove his ring
and I say *Cut it*. Later I pass his crisp
blue shirt in pieces on the floor
as I go to lay my head on his chest.

On the train back, my daughter's body
takes the place of his. When home, habit
opens the refrigerator. There —
planted on a whim in late November,
harvested and washed before we left —
his pale new lettuces.

THE IDEA OF SKIN

At the hospital
after I gave permission to cut off his ring,
they handed me a ragged, split thing
I finger in my pocket, until the day I wonder
why I spared his skin instead of the smooth
cold ring — as though the idea of his body
died a slower death than he, and was still
wrapped around me.

Time and ashes shattered,
I glimpse myself against the rain in a dark
window, feel my body raw, as if a protective
film I never knew I wore is peeled to expose
the veins beneath. In the harsh light
inside the store, I stroke piles of purple eggplants,
envying the taut skin that protects
the creamy flesh within.

Widow's Dream

My sister-in-law wears red, with
matching shoes, to the garden
party, a fundraiser for a forgotten
cause. Round tables set
with silver and flowers punctuate
the long lawn leading down
to the sea. And then the rains
start. At first a dark spot or two
stain the dresses and tables, then slabs
of water slam the scurrying guests
as they race to be among the few
under the tiny ornamental tent.
The rising surf resembles a Hiroshige
woodcut — carved blue, and green,
and edged in black. I am a bride,
moving through the crowd
in a long yellow slicker, wondering
if the waves will ever subside.

GLOVES

A thank you letter to my friend David Budbill

1950

My white gloves get dirty
feeding pigeons in Central Park
when Alice's father takes us
to Manhattan. He hails a cab
that drops us at Best & Company
to buy new gloves.
This is my first taxi, my first visit
to the store that has come
to me only as catalog,
my first escalator ride,
and the first time I discover
that something can be replaced
rather than washed.

1986

In the early light before trash
pickup in my home town, I rush
to sift through the musty trunk
hauled down from the attic
as I dismantle my parents' home.
My hand touches something soft,
like skin, only cooler. I lift one,
then two, long buttery gloves
lined with tiny buttons. A hint
of the owner's hand still lingers
in the shape of each slim finger.
I can't imagine my grandmother
wearing these. I only remember

her practical hands, resolute
in the grey dirt of Texas, coaxing
iris to bloom.

1993

Your handwriting on the lumpy
envelope greets me as I open
my door at the end of the day.
Out drops a huge pair of gloves,
mustard yellow and cream,
Willey's General Store
stamped red on the cuff. Unable
to make anything flourish
since Shedd died, I conjure
your rows of cabbages, glinting blue
beside a towering hedge of beans.
I slip my hands in the generous gloves,
remember your orderly piles of wood
stacked against a Vermont winter.

Learning to Garden Alone

I open the door to a blast of birdsong.
What else is so close and unheard?

Tiny bubbles of soap from my bottle
plop on rose leaves laced by sawfly slugs,
pearl on the basil ringed in silver trails.
Carpenter bees bumble lazily, languid
bandits tunneling the gate to lay their eggs.

I plant myself on the creamy pea stone path,
pluck insurgent sprouts,
drop them in the propped brown bag.
Scooting forward, I see a sea of weeds
I can clear like the tide going out.

Yesterday the dirty rain gouged gullies
through the silken field.
Tuesday's heat will blanket me,
the rabbits that munch my mondo grass
before I wake, the whole complicated city.

But now, the air is so clear it could break.

Still Life

Most mornings, I don't see the pillow
still fresh from yesterday's making.
On a night when the air is a thicket
of heat, I search for the cool pool
of sheet on the other side of the bed.
In this new economy the currency
is initiative. I set the table for seven,
specialize in the anthropology of three.
I'm an accidental citizen of a country
where things stay put; where I sleep
when tired. In the old dispensation,
travel meant time to be a tourist
in each other's bodies, foreign land
as background. Now, I practice
being a lover to the world, tracing
the shoulders of a new city, tasting
its breath. But tonight, my houseguest
calls his wife — *late, laundry, tarmac* —
the words like the cups and petals
in a Zubarán painting,
intimate reminders
of a larger fleeting life.

THE FIRST DANCE

I stick to my friend Alice like a leach she is trying to shed
as we walk in tandem to the old schoolhouse
tucked in another era down the narrow path
just off the rush of Genesee Street.

The sheer pitch of voices spills from the coatroom
filled with the press of kids who know each other.
Coats pile up on benches like bodies after a battle
and we file into the harsh light of the main room.

The piano player with the Lana Turner perm
pounds out waltzes and tangos with grim determination.
Miss Patsy demonstrates with Wally Matt or Eric Weber
and then we're on our own to fumble or to fly.

It's a toss-up which is worse — an assigned partner
whose sticky disappointment seeps onto me,
or "free choice" which leaves me flattened against the wall
trying to look desirable and invisible.

Even the country guys I know smell different here,
some mix of manure, raw hair tonic, soap, and sweat.
The Utica kids give off a strain more subtle, expensive,
but the frightening scent of boyflesh wreathes them all.

Alice and her partner move as if propelled
by a single mind. I watch my feet step into an abyss,
feel the pull of the wrong foot, try to dodge the arrow
of Miss Patsy's critical words, arcing in my direction.

Today, a widow at a wedding, I'm standing at the edge
of the tent as the music begins. A man approaches,
reaching out his hand. I force myself to smile.
My body freezes — always, and again, the first dance.

A YEAR LATER

Outside a car glides down the street, pretending silence.
A diamond of light crawls on the ceiling, slicing the night.

Voices bleat in my head, eating and spitting out sleep.
My breath is an ocean swell that spills on the shore.

You look past me, your shoulder shifting away.
I fold like a crocus when the sun slides west.

Cambium rings expand the sycamore, the black willow.
In the forest, a few wings wick the loud silence.

Bats and falling stars sail through my mind's sky —
that night we lay entwined against the chill.

After the service, the front door sticks on unopened mail.
In the closet, your scented clothes smell of silence.

VANITAS

on returning alone to our summer cottage

For our first meal on this high porch
we set the table where the previous owners
had left it, awaiting a future supper.
Then, the trees had not eclipsed the lake
that lay in a wash of silver beyond
the spreading field. We savored
ripe tomatoes warm from the day's sun,
drank the unaccustomed silence — until
the first truck peeled down the blacktop below.
Angry at the interruption, we sullied
the summer with complaint; timed dinner
to the general store's closing; dreamt
futile strategies for change.

But tonight, alone with my glass of wine
and solitary meal, I think of these cottages,
holding us all for a moment,
this black road, and the weight it bears —
and I look forward to a kid riding high
in his first souped-up car, his pride,
and the wind rushing through open windows
as he speeds by. I wait for the farmer, working late
on this rare bright day to cut and bale the hay
before the next rain, fatigue and relief
in the curve of his back as his tractor
lumbers by on this near dusk evening.

Even the 18-wheeler that rattles the glass before me
bears a laborer doing his job. Remembering
my own tired nights after work, I hope

someone is waiting, wanting
to slide her hand under his shirt,
smooth the taut muscles,
welcome him home.

UNRAVELING

I greet the summer slashing seams.
Surrounded by hills of cushions
that came with the house, I rip
the faded fabric on the first, exposing
acrid polyester — remnant
of some other wife. Another slit
uncovers faded fifties cheer; a stratum
of sedate stripes obscures the center
which when bared reveals pale blooms
on soft and disappearing cotton.

Threads of marriages, seams of evenings,
layers of making love to the song
of tree frogs, listening alone
to the scratch of apple branches
along the rusting screens. New lives
cut from fresh cloth. Unraveling
the image of the house back
before boards were stacked
in waiting sun, to this hill then cloaked
in wild timothy and Queen Anne's lace,
I ask — what is there, in the end,
but our fierce intent to cover,
to make do, to begin again?

SHIFTING SUNLIGHT

Splashes
on the chest
as I sand through
the archeology
of this summer house:
acrid blue, pale mannered green,
a bad mahogany stain.
Rhythmic strokes unearth
stubble from cheap brushes,
a human hair
preserved as if in amber.

What of other painters
under this Vermont sky,
this sloping roof —
memories embalmed
of bodies coupling,
the sharp sweet sting of hair and flesh
on these impossible beds?
And the dreams —
three generations around the table
in the tenuous grey
of tea and early morning
spilling our visions:
were they ours
or the remains of other sleepers
in these damp rooms?
A hair about the length of mine
slides beneath my brush.

I reach to pluck it
from the growing swath of white,
but pull back and leave it
for another hand
to sand away.

Because of the Other

after seeing Sean Scully's painting, Because of the Other

In the night a poem came, lulling me to sleep
before I wrote it down. Now, in the morning, rough
edges emerge, pieces not fitting together, raw
plates of grief sliding back beneath each other.
What I wanted to say — did I want to say it —
is that the person I became out of annoyance
and frustration and love — the one who made sure
the bills were paid, worked the extra job
so he could study healing rituals in Africa,
lay on the floor one night in Vermont
holding the dog from sheer loneliness,
stood beside him in the lingering
light of the community garden, smelling
the sweet day's work on his skin, sharing
coffee from the same cracked cup
while playing water from the split
hose over his nubile lettuces, watched
beside him in slowly unfurling astonishment
at the blossoming of our daughters, curled
into the warm hollow of his body
for thirty years of grateful nights —
what I wanted to ask — did I want
to ask it — was *can this person ever
become what she never was
because of the other?*

RESURRECTION

After reading a Dharma talk by Richard Baker Roshi

I look up *inosculate*, the word clunky
on the tongue, like something unchewable.
How can this mean *to unite intimately?* I think
of Shedd's ashes under toppled headstones
on a hillock in Vermont and somehow flip
to *resurrection,* but *rising of the dead at the last
Day of Judgment* is not what I'm looking for.
Closer might be *resurrection fern — a drought resistant
evergreen that appears to be a ball of coiled,
dead leaves but revives, with moisture.*

Back then, I peppered the world with obituaries
and death certificates, watched his name drop off
sale flyers and water bills. The fraternity
magazine he never read hung on the longest,
like an ancient mariner compelled to tell
its tale even though no one was listening.
A Value Village truck consumed the clothes
in which he knew me. I found a new address.

Yet recently, thanks are sent to Shedd and Katherine
for contributions made in my name only. Letters
begin arriving addressed to him. In the mail today,
a postcard from Gilbert School, requesting news.
I dial, inform the woman that my husband has been dead
for 14 years. I hear her breathe, type, then state,
I have entered that he is currently deceased. I say,
Yes. Currently. But if that changes, I'll let you know.

Rain

An Old Fashioned in one hand, fly rod
in the other, my father heads out
to the lawn to cast for shadows
in the lingering afternoon. The sun
on the bottom step turns
the waiting whiskey amber
as he steps away from us
to gain his rhythm. We dance just outside
the circumference of his reach.
When it rains, the indentations
in the lawn become Lilliputian lakes
that beckon to bare feet. Other mothers
call their children in; mine, her longing
parched from twenty years of Texas dust,
sits at the door and waves me out
to run through the soft, submerged grass.

These days the sky is as flat
as a blank page. Shadowless, all
becomes shadow. The air feels like a sweater
that is too tight. The roses are heavy.
Lavender lies down with the sage.
Water tumbles down our street
bearing an oily wrapper, sticks, the arm
of a small plastic doll. Breathing
sends me back beside the respirator
at my mother's end. Everything is greyed
down as though a cosmic artist
stroked a neutral wash across our picture
of the world. The fungus blooming

on the woodpile mirrors some dark
growth within me. I remember
swimming through a storm on Caspian Lake,
the surface dissolving into fog,
the sound of water hitting water
the danger of lightning.

OTHER

The time the tip of my tongue touched the glistening doorknob
our old neighbor heard my cries and shuffled over.
It's colder than a witch's tit he said, wiping my bloody mouth
with his mitten. He knocked on the door to let my mother know.
But the next day, I was back outside sitting at the bottom
of our two-step porch, feet in the melting snow
that was speckled dark and smelled like metal in the grey sun.
A few snowdrops had made it through the softening crust
along with some tough stems of last year's grass.
I unsnapped my galoshes, unzipped my blue snowsuit,
felt the fine cool air float over my too-warm body.

I heard my mother's footsteps coming through the house —
and she was over me, zipping my snowsuit,
putting on the mittens which had dangled free
from the cord that ran across my shoulders and down my sleeves.
I'm cold, she said. *You'll catch your death of cold.*

Somewhere in my body before I had words to say it
I knew: *I am not my mother.*
And from that wordless place I asked —
Do you know who I am?

THE PROMISE

The day he left me at Mrs. Weber's house,
my father said he would come back for me.
The food tasted funny there and after several days
she asked me if I'd moved my bowels.
I wasn't sure what she meant because
no one had ever asked me that. I kept
my things together so I would be ready
when he came back. I knew he was somewhere
with my mother because one morning
she could not get out of bed
even though she had tucked me in
the night before. I sat on her bed until
the men came, then watched
the top of her head disappear
down the stairs.

When my father came back to Mrs. Weber's,
I jumped on him and hugged him
and got my things and stood by the door.
He seemed to have forgotten
we were going to leave together. He said
my mother was in a hospital miles away
and children weren't allowed.

This was the first broken promise
in my life unless you count the one
he didn't think to mention —
that my mother would always be
just down the hall whenever I awoke.

SLICING THE ORANGE

Legs dangling from the table, I watch the swift
arc of my mother's wrist as she slices
an orange, juice dripping to the bowl
beneath, ribbon of peel sliding to the table,
golden sections slipping onto the growing
mound of fruit. She drops a sliver into my waiting
mouth, reaches for another orange. As the bright
flavor shines across my tongue, I don't
imagine the knife that will slip the silent
tumor from her spine a few days from now.
I don't yet know that lumpy packages
will arrive from Haverstraw, a name so foreign
there's no translation. I haven't seen
the stamped leather purses or the awkward
clay cups for my dolls — fruits of the will to master
her hands once more. And on this day
I have not yet watched her wheel back
to this table, prop her elbows for leverage,
take up the knife, and the orange, and slowly
release the flesh from the membrane
as the winding sheet of skin
drops away.

My Father's Hands

Bedtime began for me with his hands
on her back, the sharp smell
of alcohol mixing with the scent
of urine. He always started with a splash
from the green Rexall bottle, one
of many stored in the basement
where other families kept cases of wine.

Years later, when I stood at his place
over the high bed in that little
downstairs room, I'd know his palms
had been stinging, as mine then did.
But on those nights I'm remembering,
his hands slowly traced circles
beginning at the smooth base of her buttocks,
up the valley of her insensate spine, across
the curve of her sloping back pebbled
with dark moles that spread ever wider,
eclipsing her pale skin.

Sometimes, I'd perch in my nightie
in her empty wheelchair, steering
back and forth in small circles,
listening to the hum of their voices
as he stroked methodically toward her shoulders.
I'd try to imagine the place on her back
where she'd begin to sense
the press of his hand. And I'd wonder

if his touch brought back
the photo snapped at Santa Catalina
beside the trail they hiked to make a picnic
of a single boiled egg and one tortilla,
her shoulder nestled under his hand
as they look off into the mountains
toward the rest of their lives.

The Lesson

I stand on the kitchen table, its old wood cool and smooth
under my bare feet. Looking down, I see my mother's braids
hairpinned across her head so they make a sort of bridge
over the part through her hair. The eyes of the stove look up at me
and I notice the brown stain on the white enamel where the kettle
melted the night my father forgot to turn it off. It feels grand up here.

I must stand very still, while my mother matches
the sliding metal notch on the Wells & Co. yardstick
to a place on the dress she is sewing for me. She marks it
with a pin from the felt pincushion with the pinked edge.
Every once in a while, she asks me to turn, and I do, slowly,
like the ballerina on top of the jewelry box
when it's about to run down.

Suddenly, the kitchen seems very warm
and something cold spreads through me as the room
goes dark, and I find myself, cheek on table, all fluttery
inside. My mother tells me I've fainted, and I'm glad
it has a name. But as I sit up, with my feet dangling,
sipping the cool water my aunt has brought me,
the kitchen looks changed, and my body now knows
that the world can fall away in an instant
while I am looking someplace else.

April 12, 1945

In Clinton, New York
on one of those damp mornings
when the air smells sharp
like iron bars on the playground
and the first tough shoots poke
through blackened snow,
my father picked up the <u>Utica Daily Press</u>
and read out loud
Franklin Roosevelt Succumbs.

All day, I wandered
through the house rolling
succumb on my tongue
like the lozenge they told me to hold
as long as I could to stop myself
from coughing. I both wanted
and did not want to know
what the word meant. So
I sucked on it slowly
but did not ask my mother
even though we were together all day.

I tried *Roosevelt falls.*
But that couldn't be too bad,
because Mrs. Roosevelt would be there
to help him. I shook her hand
once in the gymnasium. They let us go first
because I was the only little girl
and it was bedtime. Mrs. Roosevelt knelt down
and smiled at me. She looked like my mother

but when I told my mother,
she did not seem to like it.
I tried *Roosevelt dies.*
But that didn't seem right
because he was the President
and in a wheelchair like my mother
and she was alive now, even though
she'd been away in a hospital for a while.

That night my father came home, still
talking about Mr. Roosevelt, and I could tell
he was sad, so I guessed I was right
about *die* even though it didn't feel good
to be right and that was strange.
My father pulled me onto his lap.
He told me Mr. Roosevelt was dead.
He said, *He was a great man.*
I don't want you ever to forget this day.

I worried I might forget
because it wouldn't be different
without him. I'd never seen him,
but my father and mother
talked about him so much he seemed
like a member of our family
who didn't live in our house.
And since I didn't remember which day
they took my mother away,
maybe I could forget this day, too.

I thought about the day, the knowing
and not knowing I had carried since morning.

I'd learned a new word for *die,*
but there was still something I could not name.

INITIATION

The portly machine rolls across the floor,
its girth a girdled matron.
My aunt attaches hose to faucet
on the tall porcelain sink. With a lurch,
the machine starts filling,
wringer coiling in anticipation.
Steam in the cold kitchen surrounds me,
sounds of water and women.

But it is the wringer I watch,
like a hummingbird pulled
by the petunia's liquid heart.
In time, the rolling mouth sucks in
the steaming sheets, each finished
with a lick of the sheet's tongue.

Just a touch and my finger's there,
between the rubber lips — entry's thrill,
then pain, a whirl of worried women,
a clunk as the clamp releases.
Blood throbs beneath my skin,
shame and fascination forever bound.

SAVAGE ARMS

Like shooting stars the margarine powder falls
on snowy oleo in the bowl below.

My father returns from checking the blackout,
his glasses frosted over so I can't find his eyes.

In Utica the Savage Arms factory clangs away
while tired lovers bury into familiar flesh.

You can quench a thirst, a flame, or a fear
for a moment.

One week my mother squanders her ration
to feed me my first taste of chocolate.

To be a child in a time of war is a metaphor
for an old woman getting out of bed in the morning.

The sign on the Clinton Food Market reads *Closed*
the day their telegram comes.

Beneath the ground where bleeding hearts used to grow
carrots slowly curl their way toward the light.

At the Bus Stop

Breath steaming, like cows in an autumn field,
      the other kids gathered in groups.

Every day, I walked toward the bus stop, lurking at the edge
      where I could watch them all, leaning into each other.

Carrying the cold inside me,
      I tried to smile to show I needed nothing.

      At home, I erased my face
      while clearing the table, smoothly
      taking from the right, three plates, one at a time,
      as my mother had taught me.
      An animal cunning hid me inside myself.

One morning, waiting in the country dark, I dared to edge
      toward the center of the group, big kids' legs rising around me.

How warm it was inside that circle.
I hoped the bus would never come.

What I Never Asked My Mother

I don't remember the ankles my father loved.
They disappeared when I was four
on the morning she awoke to find
she couldn't move.
Her vertical life was over
and her legs became stiff stalks
kicking out at strange times,
weights I grew accustomed to lifting.

That morning
I sat at the foot of the bed
until she was taken away.
My father trailed the ambulance
a hundred miles to Rochester
in his little black car.
There the surgeon probed her spine,
sliced out the tumor, and proclaimed
the operation a success —
he believed that therapy and time
would train her brain and muscles
to learn to walk again.

The weeks and months she was away
I stayed in the homes of friends
who became strangers
as her absence swelled.
She wrote me my first letter,
containing marks like mine
that meant she was beginning
to write again, starting from scratch.

When she came home
to a new bedroom with a high bed
she appeared to draw the circle
of her existence into a close knot
and revolve within that space
as though assigned to the spot and glad of it.

Sometimes the surgeon came
on his way to meetings in Albany
and laid his cold keys on her thick ankles
beneath the covers at the end of her metal bed.
He searched her face for a sign of sensation
she never could provide.

Silence suffocated talk
of what might have been.
No complaints sullied
the orderly progression of meals,
the silken custards, the fragrant pies.
She seemed to indulge in the rich pleasure
of friends and books, my father and me.

But today as I slice tart apples
the way she taught me,
level the sifted flour
with the blade of a flat knife,
I ask — why did you deprive me
of the gift of rage?

SACRAMENT

Washing her hair was a weekly ritual, her wheelchair rocked back
and propped, brake set but perilous as her head dropped down

in the leggy kitchen sink. I perched on a chair, scared,
reaching to release her musty braids to water

so limey it stifled suds. Blowing it dry was fun, though —
the hose in the opposite end of the old grey Electrolux

surrounding us with warm rubber-smelling air,
her cirrus hair floating freely as it dried.

Today, I brush and brush her unwashed hair,
her scalp still sensate in a spent unfeeling body.

The hair smells strong, animal — antithesis
to sterile tubes that ferry air to her lungs.

Her face softens slightly into pleasure
as my slow strokes become another sort of breath.

EVENSONG

When the blue shadow of the elm edges
across the lawn, we head to the woods,
my hand in the hard smoky hand
above me. Sounds of students slide away
as we pass the campus, and the hush
dusk drapes around us, thick and cool.
The last of the day's wasps lazily rise
from smashed apples that sink in the ground
as the swish of grasshoppers through
high grass gives way to crickets
easing under evening, calling for a mate.

Our way greys down to feeling, muzzy
light furs the edges, we're lured
by the dark that is not dark,
by the scent of decay, the sense
of a path, the loud hush
of high trees crowded together.
I am thinking of the unseen snails
curled in their coiled beds,
squirrels snuggled in leafy dreys
above us. I don't think
of what my father is thinking
in this silence that is not silence.
He and I will turn with the woods
at our back like wind, pass through pool
upon pool of streetlight across the campus,
into the house where my mother sleeps

in her high invalid's bed. He will tuck
me in, leave on one light. Out on the porch,
the smoke from his cigarette will curl

around his yellowed fingers as peepers
throb in the fated elms. The orchard
has not yet been razed to make space
for new buildings. His lungs
still fill with the moist night air.

The Small Dead Thing

I.

The small dead thing
in the back
of the refrigerator
is a strawberry
or the memory
of a berry,
a husk long lost
from sun and scent,
from fields, and brown hands
plucking the ripe
flesh from rows
of buds and green fruit.

II.

My mother's inert body,
a hulking shadow
of her lanky days,
was the furniture
of my childhood.
Could I imagine
his hands searching
her once lively body
seeking the ripe
recesses to plant
the seed that gave me life?

III.

And whose fragile son,
now leather skinned,
paces on the corner
of Old Georgetown Road,
swathed in hood and scarf
against the humid world?
Regular as breathing,
wrapped in his strange universe,
he plunges his hands in tepid water,
selling flowers
to sleek women in shorts.

IV.

The light fades
in this pedestrian room
on a summer night
in the city.
The empty page gapes
before me. The phone
rings and stops.
I am the memory
of my own vitality
as I sit here,
hiding, in the dark,
refrigerated air.

NOTHING ON VIEW

Visiting a museum is a matter of going from void to void. I'm interested...in what is not happening...in the blank and void regions or settings that we never look at. A museum devoted to different kinds of emptiness could be developed. Robert Smithson

I have finally found my calling.
After years of following

the reverberating tone
of my mother's

early departure
after wrapping myself

in yards of activities
weaving my life into lists

of good intention
instead I could have

been compiling
classifying

labeling
and displaying

my
emptiness

for all to wander through
and admire.

Before the First Knife

I'm lying on a table
with my breast
falling through a hole
toward the surgeon
who waits beneath me
like a mechanic
checking the manifold.
A vacuum probe sucks
ten shards of cells
for further perusal.

Other times, supine,
face in the glare of lights,
I listened to the snip of flesh.
A nurse once described
the stitching up as though
I were a cushion
composed of complicated
seams on the bias.

But before that —
was there a before that —
days stretched out long
and languid. I washed
the page with strokes
of cerulean and Paine's Grey.
I bought a dress and worried
it might go out of style.
I took time

to be petulant,
procrastinate.
I imagined the sharp
green of the willow
we bent to plant
for our daughter's
sixth birthday swaying
beyond our reach
in some spring wind.

Almost

You are the intake of breath
before speech, the memory
of something that never
happened. I gather leaves
of you, swirl them in piles,
till a wind steals them back.

           I dream fine hairs
on the backs of your hands —
from the clay of not knowing
I have made you up,
even as I unmade you.
You are not here but here,
the way they say God is,
your presence blown in
before birth or conjured
out of need.

           When I lay down
to give up the bloody promise
that was you, I thought I chose
an end. But what did I know
of the embryo of loss,
quickening in its own time.

First Light and Lilies

for Sarah

First light, toes slithering into the chill
of dew, pajamas wicking last
night's rain, I deadhead the lilies.
Filling both hands I toss *Sunday Gloves,*
yellow rich as cream, and tiny *Echo the Sun.*
I pause at the pale nub of the bud
of tomorrow's *Edna Spaulding,* so like your chin
as you slipped onto my breast forty years ago today.

       I'm never up early enough
to see the blooms forming, never think, as I sleep,
of their nocturnal press towards the next day's light.
But today, tomorrow's buds are already erect, *Westward Vision*
stands strident, deep black ringing an orange throat
that promises sun, and the corpses of yesterday lie cool
against my hands. Long ago, when I read *Consider the lilies
of the field, how they neither toil nor spin,* I imagined
other lilies — showy *Stargazers* that last for days — not
these familiar inhabitants of my side garden. *Trashy,*
my father dubbed them — profligate plants, littering
the world with the detritus of their living and dying.

       I think of the deaths you've known —
old grandparents, each valiant in their particular way,
Kevin and Dad, so terribly young. And I stand here,
thanking whatever power receives my thanks,
for this slime, this tumble of green and gold that holds
the moment suspended, these singular blossoms.

Miss Brown's Illustrative Materials

for Rachel

Awakening into the early dark, head pillowed
in the crook of my arm, I smell my mother,
the musty, sweet scent of the tissue of skin
on the inside of her waiting arm. I'm small,
tearing down the hall, picking up speed
as I leap on to the bed where she lies,
monolithic and welcoming. Her skin seems
old, like the soft paper shrouding
the contents of boxes stored on the shelf
above the garage of my parents' home.
In the watery morning light of a later day, lifting
the lid of a box labeled "Illustrative Materials,"
I hold overlapping years in the deteriorating
tissue. Permutations of velvet emerge —
gowns draped on the bias, folded
softly along the grain, ruched and cascading
at the shoulder, remnants of my mother's life
as a teacher, herself the model, before
I entered her world. I call my daughter,
just lengthening into the woman
she will be, ask her to shed her sweats, toss
her a dress. She slips it over her head,
her silhouette an amphora. The gown slides
in sibilance over her waiting body
as though sewn precisely for her. I remember
my mother, bending over her little black Singer
scrolled in gold, guiding the fabric with one hand
and pressing the foot pedal with the other,
the way she learned after the tumor,
when she and her heavy body came home.

I look at Rachel, in that moment after
the dress slips into place, and I see my mother,
Laurie Brown, in a body I barely knew,
rising up out of velvet, hands reaching for the sun.

What Stays

First light flows through the open doors of my dead parents' garage.
The house has been sold, I go home tomorrow, and the distant moan
of a truck as it smashes the trash grows louder.

Below the flowered shelf of the trunk lie the musky dresses
of a grandmother I never met. Ice green silk circles an improbably slim waist —
did she ease into the stitches' restriction with resentment, or pride?

Underneath, tied in heavy satin, a box from Reimer's department store.
An elegant shaded hand has inscribed
For Houston's eyes only. Otherwise, please destroy.

                                    I hardly knew Houston.
Redolent of cigarette smoke, orange stains in the crooks of his fingers,
he held me too long on his lap while he wove endless stories for his own
            pleasure.

I picture Ida, tying the ribbon, writing the message
she trusted unknown hands to honor. I head to the curb
and perch the box on top of the growing pile of trash,

knowing my husband the anthropologist will mourn the history soon to be lost.
Then, from the dark corner of the trunk, a deep blue cape appears.
I slide it on, the scarlet lining smooth with her presence.

Back to the road, retrieve the box, pull the ribbon. Spidery addresses
to James Houston Johnson in Pittsburgh and Allison Park
flow across the browning envelopes. But as Clinton Trash
churns to the end of the drive, I return the unopened letters

to the mound of remains. I think of Ida, writing
from her private place, and of my own words, my daughters,
and the lingering leaves of my life in their hands.

Meeting My New Granddaughter

Scratchy with sleep, my back to the window,
I look toward the *Original Plans*
for the Brooklyn Bridge framed
on the opposite wall and see a reflected
slice of San Francisco. This fused image spans
the country — fragile bridges, little houses clinging
to hills above the fault. Inside, the silence
of breathing in the next room, or the quiet
that is no breath between breaths. Stealthily
measuring coffee so as not to wake the sleepers,
I see a posted diagram of infant CPR
and try to envision *30 small thrusts*
by two fingers below the nipple line.
I think of this baby, her nails smaller
than the scales on the fish the children
caught last summer, that moments before
slid silver through the weedy waters
near our feet. Charlotte, a triumph of science,
sperm, egg, desire, lies now tucked
between the bodies of parents who dare not
fully sleep for fear their weight will crush her.
Yet her little lungs expand like wings,
spreading as she sheds more of the roar
and swish of her first world and moves,
breath by breath, into the hush
and tumble of life in this warm house
perched on a hill this San Francisco morning.

WHAT A PARENT KNOWS

A parent cradles a terrible secret
swaddled with his sleeping child.
Yet he carries that child on his back
riding the waves of dailiness,
treacherous and necessary. He offers
the bloom of morning's flat light
ripening into the fruit of the day,
weaves a rhythm of repetition —
waking, sleeping, building words.

Still, the secret glints like light
at the edge of an old man's vision.
He tackles the work of the world,
holds the child's mother close in the night,
breathes the smell of bread rising, until
the fell of safety is peeled back —
a staggered breath,
the wing of a plane limned in rage,
bees disappearing.

EGGS

My daughter gave me a dozen speckled eggs —
a gift for keeping her boys
while she and her husband spent
a rare night at an inn where the resident hens
lay eggs for breakfast.

In the loud quiet
after they leave, I crack one sandy egg.
A pearl membrane peels, reveals
slivers of shell, pale blue
like an early sky.

I think about eggs —
my own, spent, my daughter's,
fertilized, sealed in a lab somewhere,
awaiting a measured decision whether
to invite another raucous child
of impossible sweetness

                into this world
where every fractious day, the eggs
of our future lie spilled and broken.

Suppose There Were Light

Chartres, April 2007

Suppose you were a pilgrim
chilled beneath your heavy tunic,
your village receding
as your steps carry you farther
than you have ever traveled.
It is dark and yet you keep
walking because it is often
dark in this part of the world
in this season, in that place
where your faith resides
and is almost lost. It is dark
in the hut you have left,
and in the rutted fields
you will not tend this year,
dark in your wife's face
as you memorize the map
of her anger and hope.

For me, the passage through air
to land is sleek. My work, like fields,
will wait. Coffee steams before me.
An old man drags morning tables
into place while watery light seeps
along the east portal, washing the dark
stained glass, and a faint
French radio insists on the world.

The vast cathedral is locked
and must be nearly black inside.
Across the years I've journeyed far

and not as far as the peasant
stumbling out of the woods
onto the circling streets whose heart
is Chartres. But I know that pilgrim
in the dark: we both have traveled,
both supposing light.

GRADUATION

I don't remember how it started — something
about the pale light in the little chancel slipping
through the green glass sea where a white Christ walked,
or the welcome chill of the wooden pews and the kneeler
that clunked as it settled on the floor.
We dressed up then, nylons and garter belts. Hats —
and Sunday coats that swung when you walked.

His eyes seemed to rest on me briefly, then move on.
Now I would say I was anxious, but at the time I thought
This is what it feels like to be alive. I looked forward
to Sunday mornings then, attended Wednesday worship
in the dark.

                         One day in the college bookstore
I looked across piles of slick art history books
to find him staring back at me. Was it coincidence?
He suggested coffee — a pastoral offering?

Back then, Donne's words described my quest
for faith — *break, burn, make me new*. He entered me
the first time as I listened to footsteps in the hall,
worried about my roommate returning.
On rare evenings when he could get away,
we'd wrap ourselves in the Saint-Saens organ symphony,
drink cheap St. Andre champagne that tasted
like acrid juice with bubbles. I took communion
from his hands. I worried about his wife.

Back then, long distance cost, but that summer
stamps and paper seemed free. How did he write so often?
Then a friend wrote saying she and he
were together. He'd told her not to tell me —
saying *she might not understand*. I don't know
what I understood. I know I slid the letter back
in the blue envelope, tucked the flap inside,
and set it in a stack of letters that moved with me,
until I tossed them all.

IF LONELINESS WERE A TERRITORY

If loneliness were a territory
you could not leave, but where,
walking slowly enough,
you might encounter a fellow citizen
of loneliness, it might be good
to recognize you are both
inhabitants of the same place. Here
you could learn the language
of isolation, finger
the rim where the edges
of your solitude are frayed
and can be knitted together,
the way grandmothers
make new garments from old
when yarn is sparse. If loneliness
were a territory that welcomed you,
you could wander the land
with a fellow explorer, search
the underbrush, and, sitting
a little apart on the same smooth
rock, watch tongues of light
lick the water after a storm.

The Peaches of Immortality

Storing duplicate seeds in the vault is meant to offer a fail-safe system for the planet. Associated Press, June 16, 2006

They say a tree in China produces peaches only
every 3000 years. Those fortunate to eat this fruit
will live forever. Today, failing to find the peaches
of immortality, five prime ministers ensure the immortality
of peaches as they fill the cornerstone of a future
seed vault on the Svalbard Islands, not far
from the north pole. Through months of dark and seasons
of light, seeds, packaged in foil, will be cosseted
by permafrost, even if cooling systems fail.

Since failure's so reliable, I wonder what I would shelter
in my vault in case of mass destruction, a warming
planet, inevitable chills in understanding — maybe
my grandson cutting paper into snow with his left-handed
scissors, or lying with you in our grown child's
first apartment, her new life insistent in the nesting
bowls on the table, her night reading piled beside us.
Not the seeds, but the memory of trillium,
in a hollow on a hot day up Old Rag. And, of course,
that fresh turning again toward another after anger,
which renders us all immortal for a moment —
whether or not we eat the peach.

We Reflect Back What We Can't Take In

I gave you every gift,
blue of the spring morning,
time you didn't know how to use —
you wanted more. Louise Glück

Maybe I didn't notice the blue I was breathing.
My spring mornings were that moment at budding —
the wet light of not quite green at the tip
of the Cyprian Cedar, or the pale shoot
not yet a stem.

You may be right about time — I've raked it up, piling and tossing it,
not noting each leaf before it dried.
Yet such generous measure I've been given,
and sweetness to say for it.

My old neighbor planted a slick magnolia,
then turned to her life. When she looked back,
the tree was too high to trim. Shadows shrink her little yard
and heavy leaves rattle as they fall. But once a year waxy blossoms
glow over slow dusk.

How could you think I didn't notice beginnings and endings —
everything that ends
leaves a beginning,
even if the beginning is sorrow.

Late August, Lake Champlain

The longer I sit, the louder they become,

the offerings of this pale morning.

No blare of birdsong, no display of light

to play through night's watery leavings.

Neither chill nor warmth — I'm aware of being

aware of the seamless air.

But the tone of an unknown bird tickles the silence.

Spiderwebs wink in invisible wind.

Beyond the trees, vast lungs of unseen water breathe.

The ferry's wail floats through a muffling cloud.

Almost hidden in the green tangle of maple and beech,

A single red leaf.

GREY HERON, GREAT FALLS, SEPTEMBER

He is stiller
than still
as though drawing
all quiet into himself
leaving algae to pool and pulse,
spent leaves to crackle overhead.

His focus a magnet
the heron waits,
absence of movement
electric.

Then a strike.
Tiny frog legs wheel
then disappear,
reappear in silhouette
down the length
of the elegant throat.

How fiercely he swallows life
and its attendant
wriggling death —

envy sticks in my throat.

Conversation with Blake

Imagination is the real and eternal world of which this vegetable universe is but a faint shadow. William Blake

Imagination is fine — eternal,
if you go in for that sort of thing —
but what about a ripe tomato, fragrant
with pale green oil, redolent of the scent
of basil lingering on your fingers as you lift
each dripping slice onto the waiting
bread. And what of the smell of the skin
of your lover, similar yet singular
from other loved skins covering the mystery

of carbon and water that enables us to dash
the physical in favor of imagination.
Or take chocolate. You start thinking
about, say, angels, as I guess you often did,
and before you know it, you're ambushed
by a plan to repair your printing press, or a flurry of fear
knocking your inner night. Whereas chocolate
is trustworthy, a creamy mass softening
on your tongue, the aftertaste vivid —
the opposite of shadow.

CHOICES

*The day after my grandfather died, my grandmother ate mushrooms for the first time in 60
years.* Overheard remark

Did she forage
in the understory on pearly
summer mornings, the bright
orange crenellations spelling chanterelles,
each year's growth springing up
untouched, for the man who refused
to taste, smell, touch a mushroom.

Did she dream
of morels, tiny colonies of fragrant
cells, bubbling in butter,
while her body lay cupped inside his
in that long marriage of sleep. Did she
awaken in the hollow of the night
following the liminal smell of porcini
floating in broth, only to slowly sense
his sleeping body, the sweet
scent of him in the dark.

Would she, perhaps,
while he was far in the fields
turn to the unstained pages
of cookbooks — the pristine sections
lying flat between the rippled recipes
for seasons of puddings and roasts.

On the morning
after the first night she'd slept alone
in sixty years, did she rise early,

pull her boots over stiff ankles,
take herself to the harsh chill
of the store to finger musty piles
of creminis, umbrellas of portobellos,
little moons of common mushrooms,
the memory of earth on her hands.

JANUARY

I wait for a patient who will arrive
at 5 and push the annunciation
light so I'll know he's here. I sit
in the quiet of this arbitrary pool
in the flow of time. Suddenly
I'm lifted from my green chair
and float like one of Chagall's lovers
buoyed by the light at 4:50
that was not there a week ago
when I waited for this patient
to push the light. But now
I see the branches, see the pale
insistent sky, know that the earth
from this moment is once again
tilting toward the sun.

THE DOG BODY OF MY SOUL

Some days I feel
like a retriever
racing
back and forth
fetching the tired
old balls
the universe
tosses me.

Some days
I'm on a leash
following
someone else's
route,
sensing
I'm supposed
to be grateful.

Some days
I'm waiting
in a darkened
house
bladder insistent
not knowing
when my people
will return.

But some days
I hurl myself
into the sweet

stinging surf
race wildly back
and roll
in the sand's
warm welcome.

Evening on Barr Hill

The air chills as I step into a swale
where pines pause and red maples
reach to the moisture beneath. I want

to believe that the roots of every aspen
connect this fragile globe the way the tiny
underground stems of *Lycopodium* secure

the soil below my feet. I know that flowing
underneath us is a river of sadness, the silent
current hidden until the water swells, floods

its banks, and we can barely breathe. But
isn't it also sorrow that ties us to each other,
wears our edges smooth, and, over and over,

washes the world, leaving us rinsed and clean?

IV

CICADA

Smaller than a grain of rice, it drops
onto my hand as I sit under the oak
on a late summer afternoon. The raucous
coitus of weeks ago is just an echo,
the frenzy forgotten, and now this
tiny creature appears, white and moist
against my skin. Seventeen years of darkness
spread before it, until some unknown
calendar propels it again to this place
and the trees throb with its cry. Today
is my birthday, and I am counting.
If I'm here to hear the periodic song again,
I will be eighty-one years old.
What dark passage must I travel
as I tunnel toward the light?

In the Dark Remembering Other Beds

Even in the searing heat, as soon as shadows crawl around the day, my body
fills with chill, and vision narrows like a vise. I want escape in wine or sleep.
I'm never ready, but it's no surprise — all day, I know the dark is there.

In my grandson's narrow bed I'm wrapped in evenings he lay here
while I sang a history of his day. Guarded by a host of trophies,
I edge into the parade of nights he dove heedless into heavy sleep.

Occasional headlights dimple the walls — I'm in my mother's empty metal bed,
scritch of hedge against window. I imagine her, waiting for first light,
and someone who could walk, to wake up and bring her what she needs.

Other realms feel close. On what used to be his side of the bed,
I'm swathed in darkness and in down. How many nights will breathe and leave
before someone else lies here, remembering other beds?

Letter to a Friend as She Cares for Her Husband

Silver sage stirs in the wind
that must have blown throughout the night,
tossing the complicated flowers far
from where they grew. Here, a limp blossom
still bears its sweet, piney scent.

Across the way in old raised beds, lettuce leaves —
rosy and tender — are just cresting the ground.

As the sun ripens, the grizzled rosemary
hosts a tiny orange butterfly that laces
from branch to branch, and fat bees follow,
their faint sound pulsing as they drink and fly.

What stirs in you these long nights after so many quick years?

In the shed at the corner of the garden stand the tools —
thick stalks of rakes clotted with dirt,
a yellow, blue-stitched broom,
a spade with a horseshoe blade
sharp enough to pierce parched earth.

WIDENESS

What is this desert stumbling through me —
wideness littered with bones
I thought I'd tossed along the way.

Who knew that dried desire
would look like this, all knobby, nothing
like the petal of your inner thigh.

Or what about these leaves of things I knew,
the veins now tracing a lace of loss
that circles out of reach.

Is that a clavicle that cups
the lost rush of milk letting down
or is it your sweet harbor in my sea of sleep?

WINDOWS

Wind winds through blue cypress,
arborvitaes whap metallic rain against the panes.
A mourning dove appears and disappears
among the tangled branches.

> The curtains of my childhood sway,
> diaphanous on long light days.
> My mother's wheelchair is freckled with sun
> as she looks up and waves to me.

> One spring he drags our bed to the sleeping porch
> beneath the window and we leave it there
> until the screens are laced with frost.
> All night we're skin on skin, snowflakes in our hair.

Today the workman taps the rotting wood
and tells me I need weep holes in the sill.

PERENNIAL

Ragged anemones, rusting now,
sway in a breeze too faint to feel.

Garden in my hands, I nestle
tulip nipples deep, crumble

fists of soil to create a blanket
against squirrels and chill.

Years ago we knelt here,
or near here, not knowing

how far the wind would fling us,
how long this longing would linger.

PATH OF THE GODS

*

The metal ladder clatters behind me as I drag it
near the wall beneath the dead bulb.
It splits open before I'm ready.
I stuff the new bulb in my shirt,
gripping the ladder with both hands.
My neighbor told me that after her husband died,
the lights burned out one by one.

*

The night lightning strikes the white pine,
boiling sap and steam explode —
bark splits, needles and branches
fly across the wet grass.

The morning after is beautiful
and strange — the top of the wrecked tree
at our feet, flakes of pith on the roof.
New light in place of shade.

I thought snow only fell in winter
but all year my friend's brain
has been shrinking like snow the day after —
glistening, as it melts.

*

Driving fast on the Beltway past the city,
I end at Aarondale, which is not an English village.

My old friend's face, bright in the dark room.
She knows my name.
First the falls, then declensions lost,
then her hand in my broccoli at dinner.
Tonight she tells me she sees two moons.

*

High above the Mediterranean
fog precedes and follows us — moving,
we clear a little room of light that moves.
All is moistly quiet until a robin's call
rings out beside me. Then fog folds sound
into itself once more. The sharp scent
of rosemary disappears.
One thousand five hundred feet
above the sea, the guidebook said,
but my body doesn't believe.

Even though my mind can imagine
a precipitous pitch down twisted pines and rocks,
I feel safe, calm, delighted by the cyclamen
an inch from my left foot, the mint to my right.

        But can I live on that edge
sheltered by fog, each moment
sharp and stringent?

Assisted Living

The wipers barely swept the night rain
as I pulled in the drive at Forest Side, stepped
from the car to the click of the lock and the glint
of keys left inside where my old friend
smiled while the rain slid down my arm
and over my hand that failed to unlock her door.
I pantomimed picking up keys as Alice
looked faintly puzzled, and I, like a sea creature
twisting in pulsing water, waved and moved
through the downpour, circling the car windows,
wildly pointing toward the key ring as she laughed
wrapped in the warmth of dementia
until I stood still, chilled in the wet dark,
knowing I could not reach her.

LATE

Late to an old friend's birthday party,
I follow a note directing me to the hollow
behind the house where guests huddle
in the spreading dusk. From here,
they look hunched and small,
voices whirring like a swarm of bees.
Once, pushing strollers while protesting
a now forgotten cause, we asked
What if no one listens? Once, in a blue pool,
I grasped my friend's slippery baby
as she tried to untangle her anger
at the husband she later left.
Some husbands are still here, heavy
on the low stone wall, and some are gone,
like mine. *Her skin is wrinkled because she is old
but she isn't died yet,* my daughter's daughter says.
I reach the circle of chairs, the flickering lantern.

Blooms

We begin in astonishment —
dust motes dancing,
ants slinking through their universe of grass.

Eventually, we organize
our disappointment —
what are stories for but to gather
our lumpy lives into a bundle
we can carry?
                        But we don't end there.

One day the song
we might have sung
flies off like a startled bird
while we're building the box
in which to catch it.
We reach for a hand,
find only air.
The calendar shrinks
like our bones.

                Then admiration blooms
for these flakes of life —
light splicing the floor,
the pool of quiet
that fills this room.

MARKINGS

Yesterday, along the snowy beach, I came upon a log,
or mound of seaweed, haloed by twisting patterns in the sand.

A sense of presence pulled me in — a seal beached
on the blank span of sand, black harp etched along its flank.

Was there still life in this sleek creature
silent as a dune under the flat white sky?

Other walkers ambled over, holding back their dogs
or bending down to look in close. Comments lay

like questions on the wind — *He's gone. The warming seas.*
I see a breath — she's resting, waiting for high tide.

There's no mirror here to cloud with evidence of life. I hear
the ventilator's loud lungs sounding as I watch my mother's face.

In the night I checked the tide chart, wondered if the sea had found her.
This morning, I'm searching for something I don't want to find.

Sand leads onto sand and the beach seems bleached and bare.
I feel before I see her.

And I come to her, and stand with her. Cloud light
ripples over us, beneath a billowing canopy of gulls.

Blue Roan

Her eyes find me long
before I see her, the weight
of her gaze pulling me toward
her still presence, foreshortened
so only her head and a circle
of girth are visible. Slowly,
she leaves the black mare,
ambles toward a fence and a stranger
on a road disappearing
to darkness. I stroke her muzzle,
whisper regrets for bringing
no sugar, no slice of orange.

I know the words for need, and want,
and hope, but have no language
to discover what she longed for
as she crossed the rutted pasture —
maybe not orange but apple,
my fingers, but with a different stroke.

I think of the first meeting
of unfamiliar bodies, how long
it takes to learn the touch that feeds
our hungry places. Yet we are here,
two old souls in this slanting light,
offering what we can — my hesitant
hand, her eye, taking my measure,
not looking away.

OLD WOMAN WALKING

County Clare, Ireland

Remember this fine mist that forms a scrim
between the hills that lead to the vast
flat white that hides the neighboring sea.
Remember the comfort of the ordered stones
that cradle this one lane road — each a headstone
for the nameless hands that hauled and split
and arranged them into balance.
Never forget how spider webs appear and appear
the closer you lean in, till the whole wall shimmers
with glistening silk, and fragile hammocks
hang from rock to rock and sparkle,
even beneath this shrouded sun.
Will you remember the insistent
gravitational force that pulls you away from the wall,
across the path, past the chuckling birds that lace their way
through blackthorn, past even the blazing campanula,
to a small protected field where two cows lie in ruminant silence,
their calves leaning against them?

AFTERLIFE

After I didn't call 911 because I didn't want to wake the neighbors,
after I went back to sleep and didn't die, here is this morning,
fresher than yesterday because I might not have seen it at all.
In the street, such amplitude — an absence of movement or sound.
A single crisp leaf lies on the air, though I feel no wind.

This quiet is like the house when my husband would travel,
each object more vivid, backlit by his sure return.
No one much returns these days — lifting off as they do to other realms.
Some nights I try to find a place in the street under a smudge of sky
where the trees don't block the stars, but even then
the light from the streetlight blankets the view.

Knowing the stars are up there should be enough. Memory should be enough.
But I'm thirsty for the actual light of stars still shining eons after their end.

GHOST PIPES

I never know how far in I need to go
before the starlings' clatter pales,
the rattle of the high grass turns to breath,
and the loud hush of presence surrounds me.
But now under the clerestory of forest,
it happens, as slices of light
slip through the high gray beech.

Even though I don't expect to see them
the fringe of my sight is always
attuned, as though merely watching
opens the nave of possibility. This morning
off to the left beneath the beech — in a ring,
sepulchral, glowing, the ghost pipes'
bright absence of any bit of green.

On all the yesterdays I walked through this forest,
these icy plants were only an idea
and if I tried to bring a stem home
the fluted blossoms would blacken in my hands.
Belief lifted off so quietly I barely heard it leave.
What does it mean to worship?
All I know is that I've missed you,
even if I'm creating the you I long for.

LABYRINTH

I don't know where the mind goes or what sort of clock it has —
it's as though my brain crackles along its neuronal path
while my mind floats up with the dark bird at the top
of the live oak and looks down at poor earthbound me,
stepping over scat fresh on the path since yesterday.
This morning I feel alone and small — shrunken,
full of porous bone. I miss those inches I've lost.
To the east, the tick-ridden deer on the hill are silhouettes,
majestic and black. The doe reaches down to the fawn.

Step and step, breath, then breath, and I turn into the center —
ring, note, tiny cairn, scattered blue stones. I don't know
how this happens — I'm standing, arms out, grateful
for centuries of talismans, intimate continents of things —
and then I remember what I said this morning to someone
who called me by the wrong name. No matter, is what I said,
I answer to anything. But this is a lie. The universe,
its elements and its people, has called to me
and I've turned away.

                         I stay still, here, for a while
until my feet begin to follow the path. I notice her
as I turn west — lean and dark, her pace matching mine.
I look for her each time I round the curve by the fallen tree, know
she's behind me as I look toward the lake the fog has made
of the valley this morning. As I reach the end of the walk,
I raise my arms and she raises hers — my shadow,
stretching from my feet all the way up the hill.

April 2020

Stuffing the mouth of my mind with blossoms
whose pink is so pale it's not seen but breathed,
clutching the cuticle of moon before
it's lost in a blue no pigment could produce,
I'm ravenous for this day as I lace
my way across the street and back to avoid
fellow humans in this new dispensation.
The same route each day is a time lapse film —
clots of buds become blooms become clouds
on my shoulders. Strange, this hunger
for souvenirs of the morning. Why do I try
to record tough violets stuffed in sidewalk cracks,
the man lifting his old dog up the stairs,
the window where the blue pitcher never moves?

In Quarantine, Listening to the News

Clouds of locusts cover the face of the earth
darkening the land in Somalia, Kenya, Uganda.
A single swarm devours what 35,000 people could eat in one day.
In Washington State, Asian giant hornets behead
thousands upon thousands of honeybees, sting
a beekeeper through sweats, his bee suit, high laced boots.
The ER doctor wears a mask at home and scares his little boy.

But here's the mourning dove whose call I've heard high in the white cedar —
she's on the ledge by my window, looking in, her dusky feathers
glowing like a little fire in the weak light after the storm.
The wrecked brown orchid I was ready to toss has just sent out
a translucent shoot with six tight blossoms as small as ideas.
I've started speaking to it to give my voice a witness in this silent house.
My friends drove through the barren streets to bring me
preserved lemons, nestled in their bed of salt and juice.
The jar opens with a click. Tiny sticks of pungent rind slide
off my knife, building a hill on the wide white plate.

Now

This cold morning fierce old comforts visit —
he's cupped warm around my back and our black
cat is stretched as long as she can be
so that every part of her is touching me.
Or we harbor little bodies docked between us —
one moist, alert and milky, one, arm flung back
and damp with sleep. Then another generation
lends their pliant warmth before they lengthen on.

Now not even the person who used to cut
my hair can pat my shoulders to signal
that the cut's complete. Now air itself
is large with distance. My life could end
alone inside this house. I slip my sweater off,
inhale its scent, and hold it close.

LAST NIGHT

I always liked that monk who, while planting a hill of beans,
was asked what he would do if he knew he would die that night,
the one who said *I would finish planting this row of beans.*
Sort of like that time I took an antibiotic that made me a little crazy
and I woke in the middle of the night thinking *This must be it — I'm dying —*
I'll put in a load of wash so my girls won't have to do it when they come.
But now that I'm closer to dying, I'm wondering what I would do
if I knew I would die tonight. It would be too late to take a trip, which
although Venice was alluring and I wouldn't trade sitting on the floor
of the hut in the kraal in pure dark beyond the lights of Durban
watching worshippers dance their ancestors down, I don't really like —
travel itself, I mean — all that packing and worry about losing things,
and losing things. But here I am wasting my time before dying thinking
of what I don't want to do and that's a habit I'd certainly eradicate
if there were an instant way to do that. What I would want is to say *friable*
and know enough about rocks to name the elements that crumbled
from the green chunk in my hand, say *succulent, Lucullus,* and *broccoli*
without needing sentences to contain them. It's too late —
and has been for years before I knew this was the night it would all end —
to apologize for the inadvertent or calculated cruelties I've wreaked
        on those I loved.
Too late to remember secrets people told me that I've since forgotten.
But if there were time, I would swim naked in a cold lake at just that moment
when your body disappears and you're pure weightless being,
and if I could do this at night, I'd be lying on my back becoming water,
breathing stars overhead. When you do this, you only have a few minutes
before you're in too long and beyond knowing that. Someone else
needs to pull you out so your flesh doesn't throb with every painful beat
of your heart. But as water safety books advise, you should warm up
flesh to flesh — and I would definitely want flesh to flesh — especially

with someone I'd known through most of the ages we've lived
so that as we hold each other, we're feeling the memory
of the creamy flesh of youth beneath the final folding tissue of this skin.

APPRECIATION

These poems were written over many years, and the witnesses and midwives who helped give them birth are legion. Below, in gratitude, I list some of their names —

Marie Howe, Ellen Bass, James Crews, Rose Solari, Jenny Pierson

Jennifer Daniels, Katherine Gekker, John Gualtieri, Michelle Mandolia, Karen Murph, Mariah Burton Nelson, Sarah Williams

Friday Poets, MHFC Poets

About the Author

Katherine J. Williams, art therapist and clinical psychologist, was the Director of the Art Therapy Program at George Washington University, where she is now Associate Professor Emerita. Her clinical articles have appeared in *The American Journal of Art Therapy* and *Art Therapy*. Poems have been published in journals and anthologies such as *Poet Lore, The Northern Virginia Review, 3rd Wednesday, The Poet's Cookbook, The Widows' Handbook,* and *How to Love the World: Poems of Gratitude and Hope*. One of her poems was nominated for the Pushcart Prize.

She writes: *In my work as a therapist I listen for rhythms, patterns, hidden bits, and am witness to something fresh when areas of darkness fall away. In collage I use scraps of handwriting, stray marks, pieces of old paintings. As a poet I search for images that, when combined, create a truth composed of newly relating parts. I feel fortunate to have lived so long with so much delight in discovery.*

Photo by Richard Chefetz

Made in the USA
Middletown, DE
08 October 2022

12172095R00076